WHOOPS! A HISTORY OF BAD DAYS

BAD DAYS IN SCIENCE AND INVENTION

BY MICHAEL REGAN

ignite

CAPSTONE PRESS
a capstone imprint

Ignite is published by Capstone Press, an imprint of Capstone,
1710 Roe Crest Drive, North Mankato, Minnesota 56003
www.mycapstone.com

Library of Congress Cataloging-in-Publication Data
Names: Regan, Michael, 1946- author.
Title: Bad days in science and invention / by Michael Regan.
Other titles: Ignite (Heinemann-Raintree)
Description: North Mankato, Minnesota : Heinemann Raintree, a Capstone
  imprint, [2017] | Series: Ignite | Series: Whoops! : a history of bad days
  | Audience: Ages 10-13. | Audience: Grades 4 to 6. | Includes
  bibliographical references and index.
Identifiers: LCCN 2016031303|
ISBN 9781410985637 (library binding) |
ISBN 9781410985675 (eBook PDF)
Subjects: LCSH: Science—Miscellanea—Juvenile literature. |
  Inventions—Miscellanea—Juvenile literature.
Classification: LCC Q163 .R364 2017 | DDC 502—dc23
LC record available at https://lccn.loc.gov/2016031303

Editorial Credits
Heidi Hogg, editor; Nikki Farinella, designer and production specialist

Photo Credits
Alamy Images: Purestock, 13, Travelscape Images, 21; AP Images: NASA, ESA/Hubble,
Hubble Heritage Team, 14; Getty Images: Bettmann, cover, 28, Dennis K. Johnson, 38,
Heritage Images/Borthwick Institute, 32, NY Daily News Archive/Linda Rosier, 33, VCG/
Corbis/Roger Ressmeyer, 30; iStockphoto: hugocorzo, 29, matthewgamble27, 24, Portra,
37; Mary Evans Picture Library, 22; Newscom: EPA/Rolf Haid,10, Ingram Publishing, 25,
picture-alliance/Alexander Farnsworth, 9; Photofest: Universal Pictures, 26; Red Line
Editorial, 15, 16-17, 35; Science Source, 11; Shutterstock: aeiddam0853578919, 17 (middle
right), Anetlanda, 23, Arie v.d. Wolde, 12, borgil, 17 (middle), Dirk Ercken, 36, Dong liu,
40, Everett Historical, 4, Fotos593, 20, Georgios Kollidas, 7, IrinaK, 41, Julie Clopper, 31,
Keith Homan, 27, khuruzero, 8, rorem, 34, stock09, 16 (bee icon), 17 (bee icon), Trodler, 39;
SuperStock: Fred Hirschmann, 18-19, Interfoto, 5, NHPA, 19 (right); Wellcome Library Rare
Books: Conrad Gesner, 6

Design Element: Shutterstock Images: Designer things (bursts, dots, and bubble cloud)

Printed in Canada.
010035S17

TABLE OF
CONTENTS

ANCIENT WEIRDNESS

SCIENTIFIC METHOD GETS SILLY

The history of science and inventions is filled with stunning successes. There have also been many nutty and just plain stupid mistakes made by scientists and inventors throughout the years. Luckily, some of those mistakes have led to impressive discoveries, new ideas, and fun inventions. Read on to check out some of the biggest biology blunders, chemical catastrophes, engineering errors, and mathematical mistakes.

BACK AWAY FROM THE EDGE!

When did people figure out Earth was round? The 1800s? The 1500s? Earlier? Actually, people in olden times were more worried about getting eaten by bears than falling off a flat Earth. In the 500s BC, the Greek philosopher and mathematician Pythagoras suggested Earth was round. In the 800s, Christian and Islamic scholars also assumed the world was a sphere. Their only real debate was how far someone had to walk in one direction to get back to his or her starting point. The flat Earth myth, however, started in the 1800s—despite more than 2,300 years of common knowledge that Earth is round.

Even Pythagoras, who lived more than 2,500 years ago, thought Earth was a sphere.

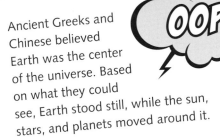

Ancient Greeks and Chinese believed Earth was the center of the universe. Based on what they could see, Earth stood still, while the sun, stars, and planets moved around it.

OOPS!

This geocentric map based on information from the late 1500s shows the planets revolving around Earth.

SO, WHO BELIEVES?

In the 1800s, English inventor Samuel Rowbotham insisted that Earth was flat—despite scientific evidence proving otherwise. He said Earth was a plate centered on the North Pole. Members of the Flat Earth Society, which he founded, still believe and defend the myth to this day. Rowbotham's vision was a platelike planet rimmed by a wall of ice 150 feet (46 meters) tall. Flat-Earthers say the United States' National Aeronautics and Space Administration (NASA) guards the wall of ice. Flat-Earthers believe NASA prevents people from climbing the wall and falling off Earth.

FAST FACT

Before Christopher Columbus tried to sail to Asia from Spain in 1492, he figured the trip would be about 3,100 miles (5,000 kilometers). It's actually more like 12,400 miles (20,000 km). The islands of the Bahamas and the whole North American continent—not Asia—happened to be in his path beyond the distance he'd calculated.

SOMETHING FROM NOTHING

Alchemy is the attempt to change one thing into another. The practice was a forerunner to the modern scientific method. A famous example is the ancients' ongoing attempts to turn things into gold. Too bad it didn't actually work. Western alchemy started in ancient Egypt. Some alchemists' experiments actually resulted in good stuff, such as formulas for mortar, glass, and cosmetics. Other not-so-scientific alchemists believed a substance called the philosopher's stone could help them live forever. These experiments failed, and the practice of alchemy was eventually ridiculed. It did, at least, lay the foundation for modern chemistry. In a little alchemical twist, U.S. nuclear scientists in the 1980s succeeded in getting gold from bismuth, another metal. But it would have cost $1 quadrillion to make one ounce of gold by this method. Too bad gold cost only about $560 an ounce at the time.

In the 1500s alchemists tried to create the elixir of life, which was supposed to make a person immortal.

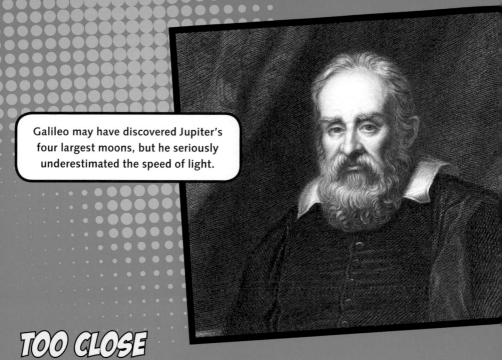

Galileo may have discovered Jupiter's four largest moons, but he seriously underestimated the speed of light.

TOO CLOSE

Galileo Galilei (1564–1642) was a famous Italian scientist. But in the early 1600s, he failed in his attempt to measure the speed of light. He had two assistants stand on two separate hills with covered lanterns. One assistant uncovered his lantern. As soon as he saw the light, the second assistant uncovered his lantern. Galileo tried to measure the time between the two lantern signals. More than 300 years later, light was measured to travel at about 186,282 miles (299,792 km) per second. The hills were way too close together to measure the speed. Even light from a lantern lit on the moon would take just a little more than a second to reach Earth. Galileo didn't have a very good timing device either—he used his pulse.

FAST FACT

Even Sir Isaac Newton (1643–1727), who discovered gravity and founded modern physics, was obsessed with alchemy. The Englishman wasted years trying to make gold. He also wrote 169 books on the subject in the late 1600s and early 1700s. He didn't publish his books because at the time it was illegal to convert metals into silver or gold.

MEDICAL CURIOSITIES

MAY I HAVE A DIFFERENT DOCTOR, PLEASE?

Galen was the second most-respected physician in the ancient world after Hippocrates. He made many contributions to medicine and the study of the human body during the 100s. But he may have had something in common with vampires! He believed excess blood caused disease. Galen thought bloodletting—cutting into veins and just letting blood flow—would restore the body's balance.

Pacemakers are implanted in people whose hearts beat too slowly, beat too quickly, or beat irregularly.

OOPS!

The pacemaker, a medical device that keeps the heart beating smoothly, was a happy accident. American Wilson Greatbatch picked the wrong-size part out of his toolbox in 1956 while building a different instrument. The device gave Greatbatch an unexpected jolt, and it became the pacemaker. It's now implanted in more than 500,000 people per year.

The Greek doctor Hippocrates, "the Father of Modern Medicine," was born around 460 BC and died in 377 BC. But sometimes he must have been thinking about the great speakers of his time and not biology. He believed veins carried hot air, not blood.

BAD MEDICINE

Qin Shihuangdi, the first emperor of China, wanted to live forever. He should have known this never ends well. His doctors and alchemists searched the world to find a magic formula. They made pills loaded with mercury, which the emperor took daily. He died in 210 BC of mercury poisoning at age 49.

After death, Qin Shihuangdi was buried with more than 6,000 terra cotta soldiers he believed would guard him in the afterlife.

DID YOU KNOW?

Ever wonder how long it would take a vampire to drain just enough blood from your body and not kill you? Physics students at the University of Leicester, England, share your creepy curiosity. In 2015 they figured it would take 6.4 minutes, or less if the vampire was sucking.

HOW HIGH IS THE OCEAN?

German and Swiss builders began constructing a bridge in 2003 that spanned the Rhine River. The bridge was supposed to connect the German and Swiss halves of the town of Laufenburg. Fine. Except Germans measure sea level based on the North Sea, and the Swiss measure sea level based on the Mediterranean Sea. They aren't the same. The different measurements resulted in the German side being 21 inches (53 centimeters) higher than the Swiss side. As construction on the bridge progressed, it became obvious the two sides would not match. The German side was lowered to match the height of the Swiss side.

German engineers lowered their part of the bridge on the right to match the Swiss side on the left.

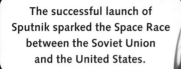

The successful launch of Sputnik sparked the Space Race between the Soviet Union and the United States.

The Soviet Union successfully launched Sputnik, the first satellite, into orbit in October 1957. The United States was desperate to keep up. It tried to launch its own satellite in December 1957 with the Vanguard TV3 rocket. The rocket exploded shortly after launch, and many newspapers labeled the attempt as "Kaputnik."

OOPS!

MEASURE TWICE, CUT ONCE

Suck in your stomach and watch your toes! Newspapers reported in 2016 that the French national railway had purchased 2,000 new railroad cars. Unfortunately, they were too wide for 1,300 of the railroad's older station platforms. Since train cars can't go on a diet, the station platforms had to be shaved to accommodate the new trains.

FAST FACT

Air Canada's first aircraft to use the metric system took a short flight in 1983. The ground crew mistakenly converted the plane's volume of fuel to pounds rather than kilograms. The plane ended up carrying only half the fuel they thought. After taking off from Montréal, Québec, it made a successful emergency landing at the Gimli airfield in Manitoba. The plane became known as the Gimli Glider.

11

NOT ON THE SAME PAGE

A little communication, please? The Mars Climate Orbiter was supposed to collect data on Mars weather. NASA collaborated with the U.S. company Lockheed Martin to build it. Lockheed Martin engineers used feet and pounds to measure force. Unfortunately, the metric system, which measures force in meters and newtons, is standard for space missions. NASA engineers failed to check that measurements were converted to the metric system before liftoff. The result? The $125 million Mars Climate Orbiter, launched in 1999, entered too far into the Martian atmosphere and burned up. The rest of the mission was scrapped.

Boeing built the 707 from 1958 to 1979.

FAST FACT

Copying someone else's work is not only unfair—it can totally flop. In the 1970s China bought a U.S. Boeing 707 with the goal of copying it and building its own airliners. But engineers miscalculated the plane's center of gravity . . . and it couldn't fly.

GETTING IT RIGHT

After a severe scolding from NASA bigwigs, engineers got the next one right. NASA launched the wildly successful Mars Exploration Rovers *Spirit* and *Opportunity* in 2003. As of early 2016, almost 12 years after it landed on Mars, *Opportunity* was still exploring the red planet. It's a testament to what can happen when you pay attention to detail.

Mars Exploration Rover *Opportunity* is still sending data back to Earth.

BABY NEEDS NEW GLASSES

NASA launched the Hubble Space Telescope into low Earth orbit in 1990 at a cost of $1.5 billion. A microscopic mistake would result in one of the most expensive scientific blunders of all time. As soon as the telescope reached orbit, astronomers pointed it into space to look at stuff. They immediately noticed a huge problem. The images Hubble sent back were so fuzzy that the telescope was unusable. After a thorough investigation, scientists realized the main mirror of the telescope had been ground too thin at the edges during manufacture. The mistake was a depth of only 2.2 micrometers, about 1/50th the thickness of a human hair. Investigators eventually discovered what caused the 2.2-micrometer mistake. Technicians assembled a rod in the grinding device incorrectly, and they slapped on some 25-cent washers to make it fit. Rather than give up on what had become a very expensive piece of space junk, NASA decided to save it. Over the course of five spacewalks, they added five pairs of corrective mirrors and two new cameras to adjust Hubble's vision. The remedy worked.

After fixing the mirrors, the Hubble Space Telescope sent back breathtaking pictures of the universe, including this one, called the Pillars of Creation.

American Don McPherson specialized in making lab glasses for doctors to use when doing laser surgery. In 2005 one of his friends tried them on and discovered he could see orange traffic cones nearby. The friend was colorblind. McPherson's glasses help about 80 percent of the colorblind people who have tried them.

The image on the left is how a person without colorblindness perceives color. The image on the right is how a person with red-green colorblindness sees color.

MESSING WITH PLANTS AND ANIMALS

FRANKENBEES

European honeybees thrive in the temperate climate of North America, but they don't do so well in tropical South America. Warwick Kerr, a Brazilian scientist, decided to breed feisty, sturdy honeybees from Africa with gentle European honeybees. He thought the new hybrids might just solve Brazil's bee problem. Kerr imported bees from Africa in the late 1950s and put them under quarantine so they wouldn't get away. Unfortunately, a local beekeeper wandered by and mistakenly removed a small piece of equipment called a queen excluder. This allowed 26 queen bees to make a mad dash for freedom.

African bees felt right at home in South America. They quickly moved north, mating with European honeybees along the way. The hybridized bees—called Africanized honeybees—started to take over European honeybee colonies. As of 2012 Africanized honeybees were in Texas, California, New Mexico, Arizona, Oklahoma, Louisiana, Arkansas, Alabama, and Florida.

THE DISTANCE BEES WILL FOLLOW VICTIMS WHO DISTURB THE HIVE

European honeybee **50 YARDS**

Africanized honeybee

0 yards   50   100   150   200

A French scientist living in Massachusetts imported some gypsy moth caterpillars in 1869. He wanted to crossbreed them with American silk-moth caterpillars to make a stronger thread. But some of the gypsy moth caterpillars escaped. The breed now eats all the leaves on millions of acres of trees in New England.

OOPS!

SO, WHAT'S THE PROBLEM?

It can be hard to tell the difference between European honeybees (left) and Africanized honeybees (right).

It turns out that Africanized bees are not exactly friendly. In fact, their nickname tells the story— killer bees. When disturbed, killer bees attack in greater numbers and over larger distances than regular honeybees. These intense insects cause about 40 human deaths per year.

Africanized honeybees will follow their victims more than eight times farther than European honeybees.

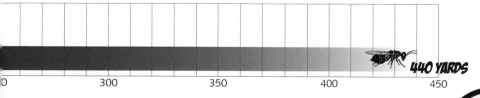

440 YARDS

| 0 | 300 | 350 | 400 | 450 |

HEY! I MAY BE OLD, BUT I'M NOT DEAD YET

Bristlecone pines can live thousands of years. Donald Currey was a 29-year-old geographer. He wanted to take a core sample from a bristlecone pine in Nevada in 1964 to learn the tree's age. But his corer got stuck in the tree. Helpful park rangers chopped down the tree and retrieved the corer. Later, Currey counted the rings. He discovered they'd killed the oldest tree ever recorded—it was almost 5,000 years old! At least the tree's death prompted the creation of the Great Basin National Park to protect other bristlecone pines.

FAST FACT

All is not lost for old bristlecones. An even older tree was discovered in 2016 in the White Mountains of California. It is thought to be older than 5,000 years.

THE CLAM

If you were to dig up a dozen quahogs—a type of clam—from the seabed, they might all be older than your granddad. A team of scientists from Bangor University in the United Kingdom took some quahogs from the Icelandic sea in 2006. The scientists froze them to take home and study. When they later counted the quahogs' growth rings, they found that one of them was 507 years old. It was the oldest living animal ever discovered! The scientists were soundly criticized for killing it. "We had no idea it was that old before it was too late," one of the team members said.

This bristlecone pine at the Great Basin National Park looks just like an average size tree, but it is thousands of years old.

This quahog found near Scotland can also live more than 500 years.

DID YOU KNOW?

The Bangor scientists named their quahog Ming. The name comes from the Chinese dynasty in power when the quahog was born . . . in 1499. The Ming dynasty was long-lived too, lasting almost 300 years.

The Giant Tortoise of the Galapagos Islands wasn't recorded in science books for 300 years after its discovery. The tortoises were so tasty that sailors ate them on their voyages home before the animals could be cataloged.

The Giant Tortoise is now a protected animal in the Galapagos Islands.

THIS TOAD IS NO PRINCE

Australian farmers in the 1930s had a big problem with beetles devouring their sugarcane fields. So they asked for help from the Queensland Department of Agriculture. Bug expert Reginald Mungomery had an idea. He would import cane toads from Hawaii to eat the beetles. But Mungomery didn't test first to see if cane toads would even eat native Australian beetles. After a couple of thousand toads were released in Queensland, people saw the amphibians quickly bypass the cane fields' icky-tasting bugs. Instead, the toads quickly multiplied and became pests themselves. Originally 102 toads were set loose in 1935. The cane toad's numbers had grown to more than 2 billion by 2011. They had invaded more than 386,000 square miles (1 million square kilometers) of Australia by 2016. That's an area roughly the size of Egypt.

Oh, did you know that cane toads are also poisonous? They may look fat and juicy (the biggest cane toad ever found was the size of a Chihuahua dog), but their skin oozes toxic venom. Dead kangaroos, dogs, and other animals that have tried to eat cane toads now litter the rural countryside. Experts have tried trapping, messing around with the toad's DNA, and poisoning, but nothing controls them. It seems Australia is stuck with the cane toad for a long time to come.

Cane toad races are popular tourist attractions in Australia. After capturing some of the hated amphibians, race officials put numbers on the toads. The toads are then placed in the center of a large circle. The first toad to reach the edge of the circle wins. This family-friendly event may be the only time cane toads are loudly cheered on.

cane toad racing in Queensland, Australia

BAD MISTAKES
GO GOOD!

DIRTY DISCOVERY

Leaving dirty dishes in the sink isn't always a bad thing. Scottish scientist Alexander Fleming went on vacation and left some petri dishes in his lab in 1928. They contained failed experiments for a wonder drug he'd been trying to create. After returning, he cleaned out his lab and found one petri dish was particularly interesting. It was moldy and gross, but he noticed there were no bacteria in the dish— the mold had killed them. Fleming had discovered the antibiotic penicillin, one of the greatest advances in medicine.

Alexander Fleming with his microscope

DID YOU KNOW?

Nitrous oxide (also called laughing gas) was used as party entertainment for rich people in the mid-1800s. It stopped being a laughing matter when it was discovered to be a good tranquilizer around 1863. Laughing gas is still used by dentists and doctors to relax their patients.

I DARE YOU TO DRINK THIS!

Danish researchers Eric Jacobsen and Jens Hald were experimenting with a substance that might fight stomach bugs in 1947. They took some of the stuff themselves, which was a dangerous but not unusual thing scientists did at the time. They later went to a party where they drank alcohol and proceeded to get very sick. Their discovery led to the drug Antabuse, which is now used to discourage drinking in alcoholics.

ROTTEN FOOD TO THE RESCUE?

An anxious farmer visited American biochemist Karl Paul Link in 1933. Some of the farmer's cows had started bleeding to death. Research by Link showed the cows' rotten hay had an ingredient called an anticoagulant. Anticoagulants make it hard for blood to clot. The cows just needed new food. But the substance found in the bad hay was made into a drug called warfarin. This blood thinner is now given to people to help prevent heart attacks and strokes.

Have a cut? Just rub this moldy bread on it!

FAST FACT

Same use, different name. Moldy bread, probably containing penicillin, has been used since ancient Egyptian times to disinfect cuts.

FIREWORKS FROM THE KITCHEN

The Chinese had a pretty good firecracker as early as 200 BC. They would throw pieces of bamboo on a fire, and the air pockets in the sticks would explode. About 1,000 years later, the Chinese made a more powerful firework. For some reason, someone mixed together saltpeter (commonly used to season food at the time), charcoal, sulfur, and some other substances. The accidental creation was an early form of gunpowder. The mixture was stuffed in a bamboo tube, thrown on a fire, and KABOOM!

China produces and exports more fireworks than any other country in the world. The city of San Diego, California, purchased 7,000 of them in 2012 for its Big Bay Boom. The show was supposed to last about 17 minutes, but the fireworks were accidentally lit all at once.

OOPS!

The Big Bay Boom fireworks display went much smoother in 2015.

I'M MELTING!

If a chocolate bar started melting in your pocket, you might not think the same thing Percy Spencer did—it's those darned microwaves! The American scientist was using microwaves as a way to power radar equipment in 1945. Then the chocolate bar in his pocket melted. Intrigued, Spencer experimented with corn kernels and a few other foods. The microwave oven was born. Future engineers made sure the microwaves were contained in a machine so they wouldn't cook the cook!

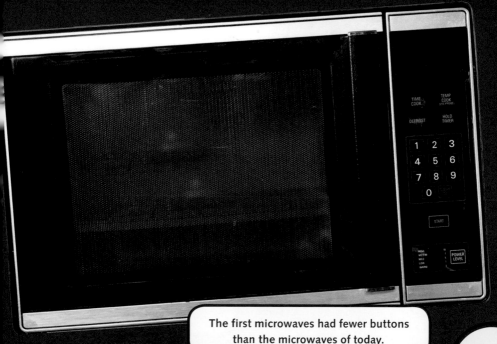

The first microwaves had fewer buttons than the microwaves of today.

25

I'LL SHOW YOU CRISPY!

A customer at a café near Saratoga Springs, New York, ordered a plate of fried potatoes in 1853. He kept sending the plate back to the kitchen because the fries weren't crispy enough. The annoyed chef decided to get revenge. He cut them into thin slices, severely overcooked them, and threw on a lot of salt. Surprisingly, the customer loved them and ordered more. American potato chips (called crisps in England) were born. British chips are known as French fries in the United States.

FAST FACT

Potato chips got stale and soggy easily because they originally were stored in barrels or tins. Solution: an airtight bag! This food saver was invented by U.S. businesswoman Laura Scudder in 1926.

In the 1982 movie *E.T. the Extra-Terrestrial*, the director wanted to use M&M candies to lure the space creature. The company declined permission, not wanting M&M's to be associated with aliens. The director substituted Reese's Pieces, and the candy overtook M&M's in total sales when the movie became a hit.

OOPS!

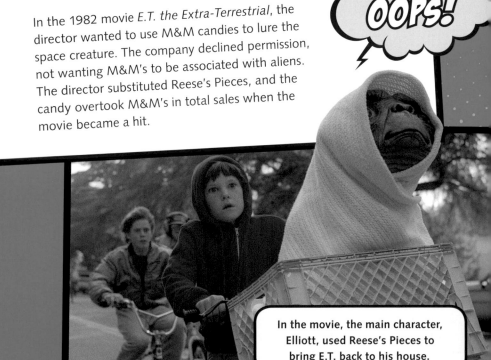

In the movie, the main character, Elliott, used Reese's Pieces to bring E.T. back to his house.

Ruth Wakefield's recipe led to the creation of Nestlé's chocolate chips.

CHUNKY SUBSTITUTE

One day in 1930 Ruth Wakefield was out of baker's chocolate for her tasty Butter Drop Do chocolate cookies. Wakefield was the owner of the Toll House Inn, located in the state of Massachusetts. She substituted pieces of a Nestlé's semisweet chocolate bar, thinking they'd melt. Except they didn't melt and left little chunks of chocolate in the cookies. Embarrassed but not willing to let food go to waste, Wakefield served the cookies anyway. Her customers raved about them, and sweet-toothed souls everywhere began their love affair with the chocolate chip cookie.

DID YOU KNOW?

The Nestlé company gave Ruth Wakefield, the chocolate-chip-cookie inventor, a lifetime supply of chocolate bars. She did not receive, however, any money in exchange for allowing her recipe to be printed on every Nestlé semisweet product.

CONGRATULATIONS, IT'S A TOY!

NOT A SPRINGING SUCCESS

At the beginning of World War II (1939–1945), U.S. Navy engineer Richard James began tinkering. He wanted to develop springs to stabilize sensitive instruments on ships that sailed through rough seas. He accidentally knocked some parts off a shelf and watched in wonder. A spring seemed to "walk" across a desk, down several levels of books, and onto the floor. He reportedly spent the rest of the day playing with the spring. It later dawned on him he'd just invented an awesome toy. That night he took it home, and his wife came up with a name—the Slinky.

Children in the 1940s were fascinated by the Slinky.

YOU GOTTA SEE IT IN ACTION!

James spent a year perfecting the toy and then tried to sell it to toy stores without much success. He kept at it until a department store in Philadelphia, Pennsylvania, agreed to sell the Slinky. It went on sale in November 1945, but no one bought it. James was certain the toy would be a hit if people could only see it in action. So he went to the store, sat down with children, and demonstrated how the toy worked. Within 90 minutes he had sold all 400 of the toys. Altogether, 20,000 Slinkys sold before Christmas that year.

FAST FACT

Kids keep falling in love with the Slinky, even 70 years after the toy was first introduced. More than 350 million have been sold worldwide as of 2015.

Slinkies today come in a rainbow of colors.

DID YOU KNOW?

In order to revive interest in the Slinky in 1962, an advertising jingle was created. For more than 20 years, slightly different versions of the jingle were used in television commercials. It became the longest-running jingle in the history of television advertising.

TIRE FAIL, TOY SUCCESS

Engineer James Wright was working at a lab in Connecticut during World War II. He was attempting to create a rubber substitute for airplane tires and army boots. Instead, he created a gooey, bouncy mess that stretched too much and snapped in two when yanked quickly. Wright and his bosses dismissed the substance as a failure. But they sent it to other scientists to see if they could come up with a use for it. Peter Hodgson, a marketing expert, saw the goo's potential as a toy. He bought the rights to it for $147 in 1950 and packaged it in a plastic egg-shaped container. By the time Hodgson died in 1976, he was worth $140 million from sales of Silly Putty. Too bad for Wright!

Children have enjoyed stretching out Silly Putty for decades.

FAST FACT

Apollo 8 was the first space mission to take people from Earth to the moon and back in 1968. The American astronauts on board stuck Silly Putty on the walls to keep tools from floating around inside the space capsule.

CLEAN YOUR ROOM!

Play-Doh was first sold in the 1930s by Americans Joseph McVicker and Bill Rhodenbaugh. It wasn't a toy, though. It was a wallpaper cleaner, useful when sooty coal was still used to heat homes. After World War II, natural gas replaced coal as a heat source. That meant no more soot and no more need for the cleaning product. McVicker's sister-in-law Kay Zufall, a teacher, used the stuff as modeling clay in her class in the early 1950s. She convinced McVicker to rename the cleaning product Play-Doh, and he started selling it in 1956. Play-Doh made McVicker a lot of money. But in 1965, McVicker decided to sell Play-Doh to General Mills for $3 million. Rhodenbaugh thought the deal was a bad idea—because it was. From 2009 to 2014, sales of Play-Doh topped $800 million.

Play-Doh is a staple in most preschool classrooms.

THAT
BYTES

THE END OF THE WORLD?

In the 1990s people feared all the computers in the world would fail on January 1, 2000. The Y2K bug (year 2000 bug) was the result of how computers were programmed in the 1960s. Those old-time computers had very limited memory, so programmers abbreviated dates down to two numbers. For example, 1971 would have been 71. People feared that computers would not be able to tell the difference between 2000 and 1900. They thought computer programs would freeze, resulting in planes falling out of the sky, massive power failures, and banks shutting down.

Computer programmers worked feverishly to fix the bug, spending an estimated $300 billion worldwide. In the days and months leading up to January 1, 2000, people began hoarding food, fuel, water, money, and other necessities. They were preparing for when the lights went off and all heck broke loose. The British government announced its armed forces would be ready to provide help to local police.

Computers from the 1960s were much larger than they are now.

Close to 2 million people packed into Times Square, New York, to celebrate the year 2000.

MEH

The big day came, and . . . nothing. No major problems were reported anywhere. Even countries where little had been done to combat the problem, such as Italy, Russia, and South Korea, were fine. Either the bug got fixed in time, or it wasn't as big a problem as many had thought. If nothing else, people got to party like it was 1999, and they had lots of leftover canned beans.

Counting from 1970, all of the 2,147,483,647 spaces needed for current computers to record dates down to the second will be used up on January 19, 2038. Will there be more panicked buying of canned beans this time?

COMPUTER BURP, POWER OUT

A small bit of computer code wreaked major havoc on August 14, 2003. It toppled the power network in parts of the United States and Canada like dominos. It all started in the state of Ohio, where a software bug turned off an alarm system. The alarm would have warned operators that something was wrong. Within hours, electric power lines and power plants were kicked off-line because of a huge power surge, crossing country borders. It was the biggest power crisis in American history.

In all, 256 power plants shut down between Toronto, Ontario, Canada, and Ohio. In New York City, thousands of passengers had to be evacuated from elevators and subway tunnels. The governor estimated 600 trains were stranded. Although the lights did not go out everywhere, an estimated 50 million people were affected in Canada and the United States.

During the August 2003 outage, 600 trains in New York were at a standstill.

Outages occurred in all of these states and provinces (red) during the Northeast blackout of 2003.

FAST FACT

The Soviet Union stole gas pipeline software in the 1980s. The United States knew of the plot beforehand and created a software bug just for the Soviets. The bug reset valve settings and pump speeds to extremely high levels. The resulting blast was seen from space by satellites.

WHAT WERE THEY THINKING?

THE BABY SPEAKS CHIMP

Just because you can imagine a crazy experiment doesn't mean you should do it. American psychologist Winthrop Kellogg had been fascinated by stories of wild children raised in nature with no human contact. He decided in 1931 to do an experiment to see how the environment affects how kids grow up. He brought a baby chimpanzee into his home and raised it exactly the same as his own baby boy. Kellogg stopped the experiment nine months later. The chimp was not learning human language . . . and his son began barking like a chimp.

Chimpanzees aren't always cute and cuddly.

These parents aren't experimenting—
they're just tickling.

THAT'S NOT FUNNY!

The 1930s seemed to be a popular time for experimenting on your own kids. Psychologist Clarence Leuba from the United States set out to see why people learn to laugh. He wondered if it is because they are tickled or because it's in our nature as humans. Once a day he put on a mask, so his son could not see his facial expressions. He then tickled his son. He also did the same experiment with his daughter. He learned two important things: laughing comes naturally, and tickling works best along the ribs and under the arms. What was never reported was if, for the rest of their lives, his kids laughed every time they saw someone in a mask.

FAST FACT

These experiments would not take place today. Scientific communities around the world generally follow a strict code of ethics. Scientists must follow rules about getting permission from everyone they experiment on. They also have to prove the experiment will not do more harm than good before they can begin.

ACCIDENTAL TEEN BOMBER?

In April 2013, 16-year-old American high school student Kiera Wilmot tested out the chemistry project she'd brought to school. What could possibly go wrong? While Kiera expected some smoke, she hadn't anticipated the reaction of her school in Florida. School officials thought she was trying to make a bomb and called the police. Kiera was arrested and faced expulsion from school. The charges were eventually dropped, and Kiera returned to school for her senior year. Homer Hickam, a former lead astronaut trainer for NASA, believed Kiera was a budding scientist, not a bomber. He paid for her to attend the five-day United States Advanced Space Academy.

Homer Hickam formed a club with his friends when he was young, and they launched rockets. The club's first launch destroyed Hickam's mother's picket fence.

Kiera Wilmot graduated from high school in June 2014. She was accepted at Florida Polytechnic University and is studying mechanical and robotic engineering.

In most cases, a faulty battery is to blame for hoverboards catching fire.

DID YOU KNOW?

Like to blow stuff up? Have we got a job for you! Underwriters Laboratories is a company that tests the safety of new products. It created a test to find out which hoverboards might accidentally explode. The test results will help build safer boards in the future.

NEXT PROJECT: FIRE EXTINGUISHER

It is probably best not to try this science project at home. A 14-year-old British student was just trying to duplicate the Bunsen burner he had made in chemistry class one day in 2015. Using an empty aluminum can and hairspray, his science experiment caught fire and ended up burning down a block of apartments. Luckily no one was killed, but the blunder left more than 100 people homeless and caused $3.98 million in damages.

ANIMALS STRIKE BACK

WHERE'S THE SECURITY GUARD?

Engineers working on the Large Hadron Collider never thought they'd be sabotaged by a weasel. But the $7 billion, 17-mile (27-km) long superconducting science machine in Switzerland suddenly stopped working in early 2016. It seemed a weasel had gnawed through a power cable. Unfortunately, the little guy didn't live to tell the tale. Raccoons attacked a similar machine in the United States years earlier. The raccoons got away, and no human operators were injured in the sneak attack.

The Large Hadron Collider is located at CERN, the European Organization for Nuclear Research, in Switzerland.

Three mice infected with the plague escaped from a research lab in the United States in 2005. The lab urged people not to worry, but we'll see how relaxed that spokesperson is when the mice come to his house! Local hospitals later cited no evidence of human infection.

WONDERFUL NUTTY FLAVOR

This squirrel's teeth can cause a lot of damage.

Level 3 Communications is a worldwide communications provider that uses underground fiber-optic cables. The second-biggest cause of service interruptions to its systems is squirrels. The critters chew on cables. They accounted for 17 percent of the company's fiber-optic damage in 2011.

DID YOU KNOW?

At the Sea Star Aquarium in Coburg, Germany, Otto the octopus found the light shining in his tank at night annoying. So he shot a stream of water at it, shorting out all the electricity to the aquarium.

FUN FACTS

*T*he philosopher's stone was a legendary powder, not an actual rock.

*T*hirteen-year-old British student Jamie Edwards became the youngest person in the world to build a nuclear reactor in 2014. He built it in his school lab and even had his teacher's permission!

*R*esearchers working at a laboratory in the United States in the 2010s were trying to make microscopic magnetic wires (nanowires). Instead, they accidentally created something called nanorods. Nanorods collect the water in the air around them. They wring themselves out like sponges when the humidity reaches 50 to 80 percent. Researchers hope to use the "mistake" to get water from desert air and remove sweat from clothing.

*C*hinese scientist Rongxiang Xu thinks he's brilliant. Really brilliant. He sued Sweden's Karolinska Institute, which awards the Nobel Prize for Physiology or Medicine, in 2012. Apparently Xu thought his contributions to medicine that year meant he deserved the prize.

Genesis was a U.S. space probe that collected some solar wind for scientists to study. It was supposed to return to Earth in 2004. But the parachute failed to open on its trip back. The craft slammed into Earth's surface at close to 200 miles (322 km) per hour. The spacecraft had sensors that should have deployed the parachute and slowed the capsule to a safe speed for landing. Investigators discovered the sensors had been built upside down.

If you were bald in England in the 1600s, medical journals had a cure for you. Apparently rubbing some chicken dung on the top of your head was supposed to do the trick. It stinks that it didn't actually work.

The Big Bang Theory got its name from a physicist who actually opposed this idea about how the universe began. Fred Hoyle thought that giving Georges Lemaître's theory a ridiculous name would help discredit it. Instead, Hoyle's beliefs about an unchanging universe were abandoned.

Manufactured chocolate chips weren't created until after Ruth Wakefield whipped up her now-famous recipe for chocolate chip cookies. After locking down the recipe, Nestlé invented the teardrop-shaped chocolate chip in 1939.

GLOSSARY

alchemy (AL-kuh-mee)—early chemistry that did not use the scientific method

debate (di-BATE)—discussion between two sides with different ways of thinking on a subject; each side tries to convince people that it is right

discredit (dis-KRED-it)—harm the good reputation of someone or something

DNA (dee-en-AY)—the molecule of which genes are made

extraterrestrial (ek-struh-tuh-RESS-tree-uhl)—a creature from outer space

formula (FOR-myuh-luh)—a combination of chemicals used to change something

hoverboard (HUHV-ur-bord)—a self-balancing scooter

hybridize (HYE-brid-ize)—a mix of two species

mercury (MUR-kuhr-ree)—a poisonous chemical element given off by burning certain fossil fuels

microscopic (mye-kruh-SKOP-ik)—too small to be seen without a microscope

newton (NOO-tuhn)—a unit of force

petri dish (PEE-tree DISH)—a shallow, circular, transparent dish used for growing organisms

philosopher's stone (fuh-LOSS-uh-ferz STONE)—a mythical substance supposed to change any metal into gold or silver

plague (PLAYG)—a disease that spreads quickly and kills most people who catch it

quarantine (KWOR-uhn-teen)—the act of keeping something separate from a larger group

saltpeter (SAWLT-pee-ter)—another name for potassium nitrate

scholar (SKOL-ur)— a person who has done advanced study in a special field

tranquilizer (TRAN-kwil-i-zuhr)—a drug used to reduce tension or anxiety

washer (WAH-shur)—a small flat ring made of metal, rubber, or plastic

FIND OUT MORE

BOOKS

Ignotofsky, Rachel. *Women in Science: 50 Fearless Pioneers Who Changed the World.* New York: Ten Speed Press, 2016.

Lyttleton, David. *Rebel Science.* London: Red Lemon Press, 2014.

Zuchora-Walske, Christine. *Let's Make Some Gold!* Minneapolis: Lerner Publications, 2015.

PLACES TO VISIT

The Exploratorium
Pier 15 (Embarcadero at Green Street)
San Francisco, CA 94111
This science museum has been called the "scientific fun house." It was designed to inspire young minds with displays of the weirdest, exciting, and most wonderful aspects of science.

Ontario Science Centre
770 Don Mills Road
Toronto, ON M3C 1T3
Visitors here participate in hands-on science activities to learn about tornadoes, cockroaches, poison dart frogs, and more.

FURTHER RESEARCH

Many scientists and inventors earn money for their discoveries and creations by applying for patents or trademarks. What can you learn about how patents and trademarks work in the United States? Try searching online or asking a librarian for help.

Imagine you are a scientist who has just discovered a new life-saving drug. Should you apply for a patent or let all drug companies sell the new drug? Look up how much it costs to develop a new drug. Does that change your answer?

WEBSITES

FactHound offers a safe, fun way to find Internet sites related to this book. All of the sites on FactHound have been researched by our staff.

Here's all you do:

Visit *www.facthound.com*

Type in this code: 9781410985637

Check out projects, games and lots more at
www.capstonekids.com

INDEX